YOU

THIS

1942

MILESTONES, MEMORIES,
TRIVIA AND FACTS, NEWS EVENTS,
PROMINENT PERSONALITIES &
SPORTS HIGHLIGHTS OF THE YEAR

TO :

FROM :

MESSAGE :

selected and researched
by
betsy dexter

WARNER ⓦ TREASURES ™

PUBLISHED BY WARNER BOOKS

A TIME WARNER COMPANY

Warner Books, Inc.
1271 Avenue of the Americas
New York, New York 10020

Warner Treasures is a
trademark of Warner Books, Inc.

A Time Warner Company

DESIGN:
CAROL BOKUNIEWICZ DESIGN
PRINTED IN SINGAPORE
FIRST PRINTING : SEPTEMBER 1995
10 9 8 7 6 5 4 3 2 1
ISBN : 0-44-91074-0

This was the year Franklin Delano Roosevelt submitted the biggest U.S. budget of all time—$59 billion, $42 billion of it directly related to the war effort.

U.S.-Filipino troops, under **General Douglas MacArthur,** retreated to the Bataan peninsula in the Philippines. In April, Bataan was overthrown by Japan; the prisoners were forced to make the Bataan Death March.

By presidential order, 110,000 Japanese-Americans were dispatched to internment camps. A quarter million miles of the West Coast were designated as an evacuation area from which all those of Japanese descent were required to move.

At the **Battle of Midway**, U.S. forces crippled the Japanese navy. The Marines invaded the Japanese-held island of Guadalcanal. Marine and army forces attacked the Japanese on New Guinea, the Solomon Islands, and Butaritari in the central Pacific.

newsreel

BLACK RECRUITS WERE ALLOWED TO SERVE AS SAILORS, NOT JUST AS MESSBOYS, IN THE UNITED STATES NAVY FOR THE FIRST TIME.

Led by Lieutenant Colonel James Doolittle, U.S. bombers made a surprise raid on Tokyo and other Japanese cities. U.S. war planes defeated the Japanese at the Battle of the Coral Sea, halting their southern advance.

On June 13, four **German saboteurs** who came ashore in rubber boats from submarines were seized by the Coast Guard as they attempted to land at Amagansett, Long Island, and the same happened to 4 others a few days later at Ponte Vedra Beach, FL. 6 were executed and 2 imprisoned. On July 11, the FBI arrested 158 German aliens in New York as suspected spies.

On the Russian front, German troops seized Sevastopol and Maikop and forged ahead to Stalingrad. The Soviets counterattacked at Rzhev and Kharkov.

RAF bombers struck the German submarine base at Saint-Nazaire, France, and the German cities of Lübeck and Cologne.

The British 8th Army, under Field Marshal Bernard Montgomery, halted the Axis drive at the Battle of El Alamein in Egypt, forcing the Germans to retreat across North Africa to Tunisia.

Chinese Nationalist armies won victories over the Japanese in Kiangsi Province, China.

Japanese forces captured Manila, Singapore, and Rangoon.

headlines
international

Their network of concentration camps in place, Nazis began to initiate their Final Solution, the systematic murder of Jews in gas chambers.

The island of **Malta** was awarded the George Cross by Britain's King George VI for heroism under constant German air attack.

The German army moved deeper into unoccupied parts of France. Crews scuttled the French fleet at Toulon to prevent Germany taking possession.

In retaliation for the murder of Gestapo chief Reinhard Heydrich by a Czech patriot, the Germans murdered the entire male population of Lidice, Czechoslovakia.

The first V-mail was sent overseas from New York City to London.

rationing of food and materials needed for the war effort began in earnest: sugar, coffee, fuel oil, gasoline, butter, meats, cheese, canned foods, and shoes all had strict consumption quotas.

CONGRESS LOWERED THE DRAFT AGE TO 18.

Washington Faces the Peace

The Army newspaper, *Yank*, was published for the first time.

Aaron Copland composed the music for *Rodeo*, a ballet staged and choreographed by Agnes de Mille.

cultural
milestones

U.S. clocks were turned ahead one hour for Daylight Savings Time.

The 1,500-mile-plus Alcan International Highway was inaugurated in Alaska.

FANNY BRICE

8

radio

Champion of Champions **Bob Hope**

Outstanding New Star **Dinah Shore**

Comedian **Bob Hope**

Comedienne **Fanny Brice**

Comedy Team **Fibber McGee and Molly**

Master of Ceremony **Bing Crosby**

Male Vocalist **Bing Crosby**

Female Vocalist **Dinah Shore**

Dramatic Show **"Lux Radio Theater"**

Dramatic Series **"One Man's Family"**

Daytime Serial **"Vic and Sade"**

Quiz Show **"Information Please"**

television

All production of home TV sets ceased. With the advent of war, all but 9 stations went off the air. The 3 network stations in New York shrank from broadcasting four nights a week to just one. By the end of the year, NBC and CBS had locked their studios, falling back on filmed shots, a few live sports remotes, and civil defense instruction films.

science

HOWARD HUGHES

FRENCH CHEMISTS PREPARED THE FIRST USABLE ANTIHISTAMINES.

Magnetic recording tape was introduced.

It was a big year for aviation. Very big. Billionaire aviator Howard Hughes and designer Henry Kaiser completed planning on the Spruce Goose. The gargantuan airplane featured eight engines and seated 700 people. Bell Aircraft, under the direction of founder Lawrence Bell, built and tested the first U.S. jet, the XP-59. Unlike the Spruce Goose, it could actually stay in the air.

The United States and Canada established the Nutrition Foundation, recognizing nutrition as a formal science.

celeb wedding

In the closest thing to American royalty, movie star Cary Grant married Woolworth heiress Barbara Hutton.

10

celeb births

STEPHEN HAWKING, physicist and author, January 8, in Oxford, England.

MUHAMMAD ALI, first American boxer to win the title 3 times, born Cassius Clay in Louisville, KY, on January 17.

SHELLY FABARES, entertainer, Santa Monica, CA, on January 19.

GRAHAM NASH, of Crosby, Stills and —, on February 2 in Blackpool, England.

CAROLE KING, singer-songwriter, in Brooklyn on February 9.

JOHN IRVING, author of *The World According to Garp*, on March 2.

ARETHA FRANKLIN, The Queen of Soul, on March 25.

WAYNE NEWTON, lounge singer extraordinaire, on April 3 in Norfolk, VA.

BARBRA STREISAND, actress-director-singer, in Brooklyn, on April 24.

TAMMY WYNETTE, country & western singer who made "D-I-V-O-R-C-E" a hit, in Red Bay, AL, on May 5.

ROGER EBERT, portly half of film critic duo Siskel and Ebert, in Urbana, IL, on June 18.

PAUL McCARTNEY, Beatle, Liverpool, England, on June 18.

HARRISON FORD, actor, in Chicago on July 13.

ISAAC HAYES, singer, in Covington, TN, on August 20.

MADELINE KAHN, actress, on September 29, in Boston.

BRITT EKLAND, actress, in Stockholm, Sweden, on October 6.

ANNETTE FUNICELLO, erstwhile Mouseketeer and actress, in Utica, NY, on October 22.

BOB HOSKINS, actor, Suffolk, England, on October 26.

MARTIN SCORSESE, film director, in New York City on November 11.

DICK BUTKUS, football player, in Chicago on December 9.

D E A T H S

Carole Lombard, actress, died on January 16 when her TWA plane crashed in Las Vegas.

Grant Wood, painter, most famous for *American Gothic*, his painting of a stoic farm couple, died on February 12.

Stefan Zweig, novelist, despondent over conditions in his native Austria, where Nazis burned his books, killed himself on February 23.

Gertrude Vanderbilt Whitney, U.S. sculptor and founder of the Whitney Museum, died on April 18.

John Barrymore, actor, beset by alcoholism, died on May 29, at 60, leaving a legacy of great film roles and a record 101 performances of *Hamlet*.

George M. Cohan, famed Broadway songwriter, 74, creator of "Yankee Doodle Dandy," died in New York on November 5.

Franz Boas, considered the father of American anthropology, died on December 21, at 84.

milestones

No one did more to buoy up the spirits of the American public this year than writer and composer **Irving Berlin**. His Broadway show *This Is the Army* featured the popular tunes "This Is the Army, Mr. Jones" and "I Left My Heart at the Stage Door Canteen." Irving Berlin's holiday hit "White Christmas," from the film *Holiday Inn*, became a virtual anthem for homesick GIs. It sold more than a million copies of sheet music—the first time this had happened in years. The song led the Lucky Strike Hit Parade with 9 appearances in 1st place. Three more songs, "That Old Black Magic," "Paper Doll," and "Praise the Lord and Pass the Ammunition" were all Armed Forces faves.

'42

hit music

"Der Fuehrer's Face," by G. Oliver Wallace, had the distinction of being the only million-seller originally written for a Donald Duck cartoon, originally titled *In Nutzy Land*. It marked the start of a series of burlesque discs using washboards, gunshots, barking, cowbells, car hooters, and hiccups.

MILLION-SELLING RECORDS

wabash cannon ball
(Columbia), Roy Acuff and His Smoky Mountain Boys

there's a star spangled banner waving somewhere
(Bluebird-Victor), Elton Britt

cow-cow boogie (cum-ti-yi-yi-ay)
(Capitol), Ellie Mae Morgan with the Freddie Slack Orchestra

white christmas (Decca), Bing Crosby

der fuehrer's face (Victor), Spike Jones and His City Slickers

IRVING BERLIN

13

John Steinbeck and **William White** both published books about their experience in the war. Steinbeck penned *The Moon Is Down*, a novel about Norway under rule of the Nazis. Journalist White wrote *They Were Expendable*, the chronicle of a patrol boat squadron in the Pacific. *New Yorker* writer James Thurber published the collection *My World and Welcome to It*, which included his most famous story, "The Secret Life of Walter Mitty." Lutheran clergyman Lloyd Douglas made quite a stir with *The Robe*, a novel based on the New Testament.

French writers made their own strange mark this year. Existentialist **Albert Camus** published his novel *The Stranger*, as well as *The Myth of Sisyphus*, an essay that concluded that the human situation was absurd. While in jail, **Jean Genet** wrote *Our Lady of the Flowers*, a novel based on his experience as a homosexual in the criminal underworld. Writer and aviator **Antoine de Saint-Exupéry**, best known for *The Little Prince*, published *Flight to Arras*, an adventure novel based on a 1940 reconnaissance mission.

books

English writer
C. S. Lewis published
The Screwtape Letters,
an extremely popular
Christian novel.

In golf, Byron Nelson beat Ben Hogan in Augusta to win the Masters for the second year in a row.

In baseball, the St. Louis Cardinals humiliated the New York Yankees, 4 games to 1, to win the World Series.

In hockey, Toronto lost 3 in a row to the Detroit Red Wings before coming back to win the Stanley Cup 4–3.

Famed bicycle race Tour de France was replaced by a reduced circuit course to avoid cyclers' having to cross the demarcation line.

The annual **Army-Navy** football game, usually seen by 100,000 in Philadelphia, was played at Annapolis, MD, before fewer than 12,000 fans. By presidential order, tickets were sold only to residents within a ten-mile radius to preserve rubber and gasoline.

In college basketball, Stanford trounced Dartmouth, 53–38, to win the NCAA Basketball Championship.

In horseracing, jockey W. D. Wright rode Shut Out to victory in the Kentucky Derby.

sports

America held its first all-star bowling tournament.

For fear the Japanese might bomb Pasadena, the 1942 Rose Bowl was moved to Durham, NC, where Oregon State defeated Duke by a score of 20–15.

In boxing, **Joe Louis** enlisted in the army in New York City on January 10. He fought only twice, improving his record to 57-1, and boosting his winnings to a record-breaking $2,265,784. On October 11, the champ stunned the nation with his announcement, "My fighting days are over!"

IN PRO FOOTBALL, THE WASHINGTON REDSKINS TOOK THE NATIONAL FOOTBALL LEAGUE TITLE.

oscar winners

Best Picture **Mrs. Miniver,**
MGM, produced by Sidney Franklin

Best Actor **James Cagney,**
Yankee Doodle Dandy

Best Actress
Greer Garson, *Mrs. Miniver*

Best Supporting Actor
Van Heflin, *Johnny Eager*

Best Supporting Actress
Teresa Wright, *Mrs. Miniver*

Best Original Screenplay
Woman of the Year,
Michael Kanin and Ring Lardner, Jr.

Best Adapted Screenplay
Mrs. Miniver, George Froeschel,
James Hilton, Claudine West, and
Arthur Wimperis

Best Director
William Wyler, *Mrs. Miniver*

hit movies of 1942

1. *Bambi* Walt Disney Studios ($7,265,000)

2. *Mrs. Miniver* MGM ($5,390,000)

3. *Yankee Doodle Dandy*
   Warner Brothers ($4,719,000)

4. *Random Harvest* MGM ($4,665,178)

5. *Casablanca* Warner Brothers ($4,145,178)

top 10 box-office stars

1. Abbott and Costello
2. Clark Gable
3. Gary Cooper
4. Mickey Rooney
5. Bob Hope
6. James Cagney
7. Gene Autry
8. Betty Grable
9. Greer Garson
10. Spencer Tracy

movies

The Pride of the Yankees, a film biography of
Lou Gehrig, starred Gary Cooper and Babe Ruth.

Continuing their string of successful
"road" movies, Bing Crosby and Bob Hope
teamed up once more with Dorothy Lamour
in **The Road to Morocco.**

BETTY GRABLE

cars

In February, by order of the government, automakers halted production of civilian passenger cars. All automaking facilities—including men and machines—were placed entirely at the disposal of the war program. Conversion of factories and equipment and training were vigorously carried out on a 24-hour-a-day schedule. March 2, the rationing program for new passenger cars was inaugurated, establishing a system of eligibility classifications. Those considered having the greatest need for new cars were as follows:

In May, the national speed limit was set at 40 mph. It was later cut back to 35.

Military service and rationing put many autos in storage for the duration of WWII. Chrysler spent $40 million to increase tank production and started a huge aircraft engine plant in Chicago.

1. *Doctors, veterinarians, and visiting nurses*
2. *Ambulance services*
3. *Ministers*
4. *Firefighters*
5. *Police*
6. *Public health and safety workers*
7. *U.S. mailmen*
8. *Taxicab services*
9. *Highway construction and repair workers*
10. *War plant executives and workers*

SAVE
STEPS, TIME and TIRES

DRESSING UP WAS *DÉMODÉ*. OSTENTATION WAS CONSIDERED SELFISH AND UNPATRIOTIC.

There was great reliance on multiple-purpose clothing, with dresses cut to look like jackets or bolero suits, and late afternoon dresses that doubled as evening gowns. Any skirt fullness was gathered into a lowered waistline at the front and seaming carried the eye down to the hem, creating an illusion of length. Hip seams and large, low hip pockets with belts slotted through them were used to break the austere lines of coats. Big sturdy coats were either back-belted and double-breasted, or swung wide, like tents, from padded shoulders.

shopping spree

tintype taffeta dirndl **$12.95**

debutante coat **$21**

man's overcoat **$45**

child's ski suit **$6**

man's pigskin gloves **$3.95**

overnight case (21") **$26.50**

daytime dress (wools and crepes) **$10.00**

woven silk or moiré tie **$3.50**

black rayon crepe square-neck dress **$12.95**

fashion

Ingenuity turned necessity into creative opportunities. Cords and strings of beads were used instead of elastic to hold hats in place. Tea was used instead of dye to color shirts. Wool linings and decorative flaps and pockets were banned—but fur linnets were permitted and unrationed sequins and braid adorned suits.

22

Bonwit Teller

NEW YORK · WHITE PLAINS

Blotta's sure hand has caught the note of the year. A black wool
dusted with rabbit's hair. Simple and slim as a Chinese jade. Shadows
of black cotton-velvet around the Chinese neck closure and at the
wrists, 69.95   Little point-crowned Chinese hat in black silk velvet, 30.00

Misses' Dresses...Custom Millinery, both Sixth Floor

BONWIT TELLER, FIFTH AVENUE, NEW YORK · WHITE PLAINS

final
factoid

The Women's Army Auxiliary Corps (WAAC) was established by act of Congress.

credits

archive photos: inside front cover,
pages 1, 2, 15, 20, 24, 25, inside back cover

associated press: pages 3, 5, 6, 10, 16

photofest: pages 8, 18, 19

photo research:
alice albert

coordination:
rustyn birch

design:
carol bokuniewicz design
paul ritter

'42